Perfect Blemishes

From my Closet

Angelita Bacchus

Roselle, New Jersey

Copyright © 2023 by Angelita P Bacchus

All Rights Reserved.

No portion of this book may be reproduced in any form without written permission from the publisher or author, except as permitted by U.S. copyright law.

This is a work in nonfiction. This book was taken from the author's personal experiences, her memoir captured important segments from her life. Some names and identifying details of people described in this book have been altered to protect their privacy.

For more information contact:
Independent Authors Publications
PO Box 7062,
Roselle, NJ 07203
www.independentauthorspublications.com

Cover Design – Webprint Lab
Edited – Catherine Felegi
Formatting – Polgarus Studio

Print ISBN: 978-1-950974-12-2
Digital ISBN: 978-1-950974-13-9
Library of Congress Control Number: 2023902266

I would like to dedicate my book to women.

To the woman who allowed her experiences to cripple her life instead of using these situations to propel her towards her breakthroughs. Wearing those scars as a necklace is a great punch in the face of life's adversities.

To the woman who made every choice to love everyone else except herself. Learning to put you first is a hell of a tool - it's not selfish. It's needed. Start setting boundaries and draw a line in the sand. You deserve to be loved.

Finally, my mom. She was a perfect example of struggling, overcoming and growing as an individual. She didn't have a lot of money, but she always provided for us. Her mission to end generational curses was embedded in finding the love of Jesus Christ. With no high school diploma, she was able to get through theological school. From an evangelical role, she was ordained as a pastor and had a small church. This woman faced demons with or without fear and trusted God all the way. I'm convinced depression and diabetes got the best of her physical weaknesses, but we will meet again in the Promise Land. That's where we'll get to celebrate our losses on this side and our gains on the other side. Our goal is to keep the faith and fight on.

Depression is real. Remember, God is more real. I empathize with and relate to anyone who's experiencing this giant in the room. Learn from other people's mistakes and never give up on living. God does not need my help to end my life. He needs my obedience to live the life he blessed me with.

Contents

Introduction 1

1. Scattered 3

2. New Beginnings 15

3. Sister, Sister 21

4. Reflections 25

5. Broken 33

6. Emotions and Betrayal 45

7. Let's rewind… 51

Summary 65

Daily Diary 69

Introduction

This book is mainly for women. We are strong beyond measure and I am convinced that we go through so much more than men. According to society, we are supposed to be the weaker vessel. On the contrary, we perform so many successful roles as females, that thought process boggles me. I truly believe we were not created to carry all of the burdens life sends our way. Nevertheless, it's my bizarre opinion that Jehovah placed an extra rib in us because He knew we were going to need it. Adam ain't got anything on us –he's actually missing a rib!

The following short stories were written from selected segments of my life. I repeated some of my writings because short stories can be read separately. My goal is to help others by sharing parts of my journey. Some might judge me, but it's okay; none of us are perfect. This is an updated version since I released a copy back in 2018. For personal reasons, I decided to re-write some parts and as a result, I was able to include my Prison Love story.

However, it's the trials and processes we have to endure that allow us to see the perfect plan Jehovah has for us. Nothing takes our God by surprise; I don't imagine Him in Heaven running around at the twelfth hour trying to cook something up to help us. The book of Jeremiah, 1:5 states, "Before I formed thee in the belly, I knew thee, and before thou came forth out of the womb, I sanctified thee…."

Of course, we don't all believe in God or the Bible, but that's a whole new book in of itself. The central theme of these short stories is simply, LET GO AND LET GOD. We can't fix everything, we can't know it all, and we surely can't pass the test every single time. I always heard this saying as a child, and the meaning really became evident when I became an adult - "Losing one or two rounds doesn't mean we have to LOSE THE FIGHT."

We must take the lessons we learn along the way and share them to help others. Don't ever be ashamed of who you are or what you've been through. Someone else is waiting to hear your message. This is my life, it's my walk, and they are my Perfect Blemishes.

1. Scattered

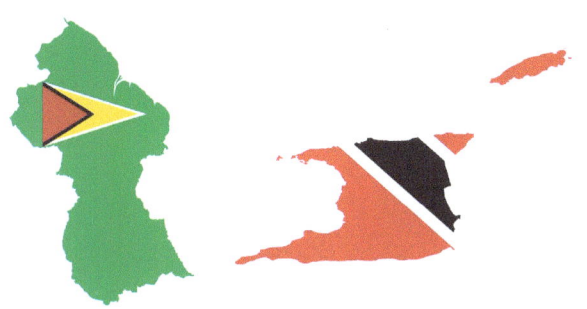

I was born and spent the first seven years of my life in Guyana, South America. Later, in my seventh year, I migrated to Trinidad and Tobago. Life was vastly different living in Guyana. I lived with my grandmother, and we had our own home in a residential neighborhood located in Roxanne Burnham Gardens where she raised my two brothers and me.

Daily, we made wonderful memories. It was truly a place we could call home. After all, it was what we knew. My grandmother was the only one who took care of us. In fact, it wasn't until I was seven years old that I met my mom for the first time. I remember that moment as if it happened only a week ago.

I was in the yard playing with my siblings when I looked over the fence and saw this strange woman. She had a pleasant look on her face, but for me, trusting a stranger was forbidden. So I ran into my home and called my granny. "Granny, Granny! There's a strange woman outside coming into the yard!" Just then, my eldest brother said, "It`s Mother." I remember thinking, *Granny is my mother, not this strange woman.*

Soon, my grandmother gathered us in the living room where she and the strange woman sat down to explain everything to me. I, being the youngest, felt completely lost. This new woman, whose name was Heather, was less of a stranger to my brothers, Bryant and Gavin, and they adapted easily. In my mind, Granny was my mother and no one else could ever take her place.

It was difficult and definitely took some time for me to adjust to this stranger being my mom, but eventually, I started getting used to it. A few weeks later, I learned that my new mom had plans to take us from the only home I ever knew to another home located in another country.

This was beyond insane to me. How could she do this to us? How could my Granny be so willing to give us to this strange woman? This was much harder for me to digest, but I had no say in the matter. I was only seven and I couldn't make my new mom leave me with Granny, so I had to do what I had to do. My grandmother sent my eldest brother, Bryant, to live with my mother for about two months before my other brother, Gavin, and I joined him. Then, the day came when we migrated to the beautiful island of Trinidad and Tobago. I didn't know it at the time, but my feelings were actually mixed.

I was happy to be reunited with Bryant, and to still have Gavin as well. Being the baby and the only girl had its perks, and I needed both of my brothers in my life now more than ever. In essence, I had a sister named Natasha, whom we called Natty. She was not my mother's child, but we all shared the same father. Although I was a bit happy, sadness was also present because I missed my real home and Granny - the only mother I knew.

Almost everyone I knew was now just a part of my past. All I had to look forward to was newness. Adjusting was definitely a process. When we left the Piarco International Airport in Port-Of-Spain, Trinidad, West Indies, Mom took us to a place where we were introduced to a strange man named Mr. David. Later, I learned he was her boyfriend and we were staying with him in his home, not her own. Mother took care of all the necessary things for us like school, clothing, and transportation.

A few weeks later, we were ready for school and moving forward in our new lives. It was difficult coping with the new system. The children were not all that nice. My brothers and I were placed in separate schools. Based on circumstances and timing, we had to be split up. Bryant was old enough for high school. However, Gavin and I were still in elementary school. There weren't any schools that would take both of us, so we too had to attend separate schools. After nearly five months, we were forced to move to another place. My mom broke up with Mr. David, and she decided to take us to a place called Morvant.

There were no other words to describe this new place outside of horrible. Trinidad, as a whole, is a beautiful island. However, our side of town was poor and outdated. My grandmother's home was the best, not only because it was my first home, but the living conditions were much more pleasant. With Granny, we had a private home with a big backyard. My mom`s boyfriend's home was smaller and had no backyard since it was public housing, but at least I could say it was clean.

This new place that we were forced to live in was no comparison to anything we'd known before. Our home was a wooden house with two bedrooms and no in-house bathroom facilities. We had an outdoor bathroom with a toilet that originally was a shed and a latrine. We had a Latrine not a toilet. It was a 6-7 feet hole in the ground (we had a room built around it for privacy. Latrines are not able to flush after using the bathroom so the smell was bad. We used Pitch Oil to try and decrease this unpleasant odor. Our bathroom was built with galvanize and a concrete flooring. , we had to fetch water from a tank in order to use a bucket to bathe. In fact hot water from the stove helped me to avoid cold showers. So many mornings I dread taking baths but it was my only option and I took some time to get use to it.

The kitchen sink used PVC pipes to send the water outside a hole in the wall. Kind of like the way an Air condition would functions. We got water from aa neighborhood standpipe that was located in a nearby cemetery. My brothers mainly had the task of fetching water only sometimes I had to help them. The goal was to fill a 500-gallon tank for daily usage.

Only two bedrooms so me and my siblings shared one room. That was challenging at times they had to leave the room when I requested to use it Privately. Cooking and television, I think I mentioned it later on in another chapter. We used a car battery for the TV Power and a physical gas tank with a hose to get the stove to work. My life changed dramatically when we moved to Morvant.

Later on, we got a new restroom that functioned normally, but the home was too small to hold it all in one. Therefore, we always had an outdoor restroom facility. It was by the Grace of God that our home stayed standing when there was storms etc because the structure was poorly built. I walked on dirt roads and hilly steep roadways. It was Slippery and hard to walk when it rained. Laughter became our medicine when anyone fell. Once there was no major injuries we made fun of each other. I remember my mom fell and she quickly got up. She was more concerned on who saw her fell and not so much of was she in pain. This was our life, the homes and total environment reminded me of a shantytown.

We had a difficult time living - a few neighbors faced the same problem we coped with because poverty was predominant in that neighborhood. Overall, Morvant was not a bad place to live. It was just a different world. We were residing on squatter's land. The only other option would be to become homeless. My mother worked hard, and I knew she wanted to give us better, but the outcome only produced the worst. I wanted to go back to Guyana, but that was not an option. Mother said my grandmother was tired and she needed to rest. She also said it was now her time to play the mother's role, which she neglected for so many years.

My mother was married at the age of fifteen and was divorced by the age of twenty-two. All she knew was how to sing and how to cook. Cooking became her way of making an income since singing didn't work for her. Now, she knew how to sing, and Mother was amazing, but she just never got that big break. There was a time in her life when my mother sang in clubs and did lots of gigs with her group. But, after living in places like Suriname and Barbados, she decided to return home and took on the role of being a single parent She had to be both mom and dad, with no help – not even from Granny, since we lived in another country. Working as a cook did not bring in much, but we made it work.

Being that we were squatting living illegally in the country, we had no rights to the land that we lived on. On several occasions, many neighbors, including us, had our homes torn down by government officials. Every time our home was destroyed, we had to build it back. This became a regular part of my life, and it was a bitter part we dealt with. Since our homes were built from wood, it was doable to rebuild it in a week or less.

Meanwhile, we lived in a house that was either open or halfway built. The roof was missing some nights, so we prayed it did not rain before we rebuilt. This happened for approximately two years, around three to five times. Finally, I think the government officials got tired and stopped coming. I guess it became clear to them that we had no other options and we had to live somewhere. We were so poor, our stove functioned with a gas tank. Our television was black and white and operated with a square car battery. Whenever the power was low, my brothers would need to purchase a new battery and gas tanks so that we could cook and watch television.

Later on, after saving up, my mom was able to replace our outdated facilities with modern-day equipment. These aspects of my life made me stronger. As I grew older, I adapted. It was not easy to cope with, but it was my life. Unfortunately, these circumstances affected my siblings differently. By 1987, both of my brothers dropped out of school. Peer pressure got the best of them. Their schools became more and more difficult. They dealt with not only being teased for our living conditions, but also for our accents.

It was clear to many that we spoke differently since our native land was Guyana and not Trinidad and Tobago. We stood out like a sore thumb.

I was also bullied, but I pushed through. Although I was the baby and a girl, mentally, I was much stronger when it came to peer pressure. While I attended the Bethlehem Girls RC School every Friday, I would be challenged. They nicknamed me the FRIDAY BOBOLEE. I remember them saying, "All for one, and one for all," as they formed a circle with me in the middle.

My principal would counsel me and have meetings with the bullies' parents, but that didn't work. One day, I was done! The girls were doing their regular bullying – telling me I didn't fit in, saying they would never play with me, hitting me, and pulling my hair. I grabbed one of the girls teasing me and slammed her head into the concrete staircase. We fought for a good minute before a teacher came and separated us. As I was walking to the principal's office, I felt fear. The principal took me into the office and told the other student to go sit with a teacher. To my surprise, my principal shook my hand and said, "It was time." She said, "I watched you be bullied daily. Sometimes, you have to do what you have to do." From that day on, I was respected. Eventually, the fear subsided and I was accepted as one of the girls.

My mother allowed my brothers to quit school when it became too tough. I guess she had other things to focus on, like being a mother and a father for us. When poverty and other circumstances play a role in a person's life, they either find strength from it and are able to defeat the odds, or become completely debilitated. Unfortunately, the latter was the case with my two brothers, and ultimately, they gave up.

I, however, was determined to do something different, so I chose to overcome my obstacles. I completed high school and found a way to beat the odds. There were many days I had no idea how I would make it through, but it only made me stronger. My mother did her best. She was a fifteen-year-old bride, and her mother allowed that to happen by signing her daughter's marriage license.

During her seven-year marriage, my mom endured several accounts of infidelity and mental abuse. She was an army wife. Her husband, Gary Paton, was a general in the Guyana Defense Force. He was tall, dark skinned, and extremely attractive. Due to his job title and good looks, he was a magnet to other women, who were all too eager to do whatever he wanted. Mother knew her husband was having outside relations. At times, she had to fight other women off, even while pregnant, since the other women saw her as a threat. Gary would also drink and drive, damaging vehicles and property, leaving the family with no money to spare. The other army wives knew and would gossip, causing pure embarrassment. Finally, they agreed to separate. In 1975, I was conceived in the middle of a legal separation case with another man, sealing my mom's divorce.

It took many years for the truth to surface. When I turned seventeen, sometime in the summer of 1992, my mother received a letter. She said it was from my godfather. I was so excited to know someone who lived in America. Back then, knowing someone from America was cool, so I took his picture to my friends. They all agreed we both looked alike, though I told them I didn't think we were related. During those years, I attended high school and I was a member of the Morvant Laventille Secondary School Steel Orchestra. I played with MLSS band for about five years. These were some of the best days I'd ever had.

One day after preparing for a summer festival, I went home to eat my favorite food - okra and rice. After fixing my plate, Mom sat me down and poured out her heart. She told me of all the marital issues, the ups and downs she faced with her ex-husband who I thought was my father up to that day. However, I was sadly awakened when I learned he was not my dad. I was actually the seed of the man I'd always known as my godfather.

I was a product of infidelity. My existence was the elephant in every room. Up to this point in my life, I had three siblings - two brothers and my sister, Natty. In reality, I lost her as a sister, since we did not share the same father anymore, though in my mind, Natty will always be my sister. I realized I did not share parents with the siblings I loved so dearly. They were my mom's ex-husband's children and I belonged to my godfather. It was clear why we did not look alike and why I felt like I was adopted, why my friends thought I looked like that man in the picture.

As I reminisced, I concluded my mother loved us all, but I reminded her of her past and hidden secret, the one that helped to erase her marriage.

To this day, I believe seeing me each day was like an open wound Mom carried for over 17 years. And confessing the truth to me allowed her to heal, even though it affected me negatively.

My mother and I never had a great relationship. There were times when we had major arguments, and she used corporal punishment as the norm when dealing with me. I got the most beatings out of my brothers, and was required to do the most housework because, as she put it, I was female. In fact, I had to clean up after my brothers, even if it wasn't my mess, or I would get more beatings. My brothers were favored more , they got everything they wanted , they got to hang out while I was a loner, since a woman's place is at home. They were a few sexist teachings now that I am older I see it that way. Beatings was an option for them but I got what ever was available, pot covers. Slippers etc.

Sometimes she spared me only to add all the wrath into one general beating to circumvent for the times she let me off the hook

Some days, I felt adopted due to the way she treated me, and because I looked more like my birth father than the rest of my family. I felt like I couldn't love her the way she may have deserved, especially after hearing she lied to me for so many years. My pain and disappointment barred us from having a better mother and daughter relationship. However, we made the best of it and that's all we could do.

Life back then seemed normal, but looking back now, I realize I was abused. I was depressed and dealing with it alone because no one understood me. Of course, I am unable to diagnose myself, but if I knew what I know now, all my symptoms were related to some form of depression.

In essence, Mom wanted the best for me, but her approach wasn't always helpful. She loved to cook - that was her trade. However, she wanted better for me, so she pushed me away from doing that. I remember her saying, "You would be more than a COOK - stay focused on your schoolwork."

On the one hand, I was a rebellious child who always spoke up and expressed myself. These expressions only led to beatings that went on for a few years. Why was I expected to stay at home while the guys roamed? Why was I told to clean up the home simply because I was the female? Mom would make Bryant and Gavin weed the grass and do other outside chores, but too many times, the home was mine to clean. I felt they should have helped too, but the outcome was always an argument, which then led to a whipping.

Fast forward, after talking to my new dad for some time – or I should say, my real dad – we began to develop a relationship. About three years later, my mother helped me apply for my U.S. visa because my biological father wanted me to move to the United States. We had to go through the normal process, Back then a DNA test that was required, but finally, everything was set and I got my legal permanent residence.

Mother supported me through high school, and she sacrificed a lot because of it. There were days she wore flip flops and refused to buy a proper shoes to ensure she could buy my books and uniform for school. In 1992, I graduated with my CXC Certificate from Morvant Laventille Secondary School. I was grateful to have had a mother like her. Even though all the past pain created a wedge, I was appreciative of the love she showed me in spite of our ups and downs.

2. New Beginnings

In 1995, I migrated to the U.S.A.. Coming to America was an exciting event for me. When I got here, I didn't know what to expect. My dad was married to another woman, and I had new sisters and brothers. It took me years to connect with them, and to this day, we have a cordial relationship.

I started working for Duane Reade Pharmacy as a cashier one month after I came to the U.S. before moving on to a better career with HSBC Bank. During my years as a cashier, I met a young lady named Davila. She and I became good friends. Not too long after our friendship began, she introduced me to a young man name R-Jay.

Instantly, I felt a strong attraction to him. It didn't take long for us to become more than acquaintances. We skipped the friendship phase and he became my first real boyfriend. Yes, you read that correctly. I was twenty years old before I ever dated anyone. Unfortunately, what I thought was amazing turned out to be much more complicated. He was married!

Had I known that in the beginning, I would have never gotten involved with him. However, I had no idea. He made sure to keep me away from his family, telling me they were racist. R-Jay is a Native Guyanese mixed with East Indian and I am Black, so he led me to believe that his family would never accept me. Therefore, it was easy to keep that vital information from me. I believed him for over a year.

I would go on to find out that his wife lived in another country. I'm not sure if Davila knew he was a married man, but shortly after, she became my enemy, I am not sure if she knew he was married but her behavior says a lot of guilt. She even went as far as to curse me out. In her words, I was a whore because I lost my virginity to R-Jay. I had fallen in love with him and it seemed like the right thing to do. It hurt me that Davila no longer wanted to be my friend, but I couldn't allow it to make me bitter. Besides, I was in love.

From the beginning, R-Jay played me. I mean, he played me good. I lost my friend, and moved on no longer a virgin and blindly in love with a married man. One day, the truth finally came out, but not before I became pregnant with my first child. At the age of twenty-two, I became pregnant with a married man's child.

Neither his wife nor I knew of each other. In fact, to me, this was a picture-perfect family. My first love and I were going to welcome our first child. It felt like all new beginnings, but it was pending a not-so-happy ending. Quickly, what started out as a perfect picture became a horrifying nightmare. The nine months I should have been happily waiting on the arrival of my child were days and nights filled with shame and sorrow. This man, the one who I thought loved me as much as I loved him, did not want his child. He offered to pay for me to get an abortion and I quickly told him no.

Being a Christian, that was not an option for me. I get the fact that Christians also shouldn't fornicate and have babies out of wedlock. However, two wrongs don't make a right. I was taught to never cover an issue with another issue; you just deal with it. I was having my baby and had planned to survive the best way I knew how. Sometime during my second trimester, R-Jay showed up asking to borrow some money. He said it was to pay for damages to his uncle's car and, being the fool I was back then, I gave him the money. Our daughter is a college grad now. Ask me if I ever got that money back.

Once, I did receive a phone call from someone who asked if I knew R-Jay was married. She didn't leave a name or anything, so I was skeptical. When I confronted R-Jay, he blatantly denied it and reassured me that whoever it was just didn't like me because I was Black. Being young, dumb, and lacking experience about relationships, I fell for his lies. In my eyes, he told the truth and everyone else were just liars who didn't want us to be together. One day soon, I would learn the sad truth.

I named my beautiful baby girl KayKay. She was gorgeous and so sweet. We really didn't need R-Jay. However, since I had been robbed of a father's love because of infidelity, I didn't want KayKay to miss out on a father's love because of my stupidity. Funny how history repeats itself. My mom messed up and had me at twenty-three years old, and here I was at almost twenty-three and I unknowingly repeated her same mistake. My mom knew very well what she was doing was wrong, but she did it as a coping mechanism to help deal with her disappointment. I, on the other hand, had no clue I was an adulterer until well after I'd brought another life into this world. Either way, my life mimicked hers and it wasn't positive.

One day, I called R-Jay and his new girlfriend's mom picked up the phone. We spoke for a moment. She thought I was R-Jay's wife making an overseas call from Guyana. When I explained to her that I was living right here in the U.S., she was surprised. She told me to call her back after speaking to R-Jay, so I did. It was clear then that R-Jay was married and I was being mistaken for his wife.

Finally, after all this time, R-Jay confessed. As he was speaking, I remembered that day when I was at his home and I saw some baby clothes in his closet. Of course, he lied. And clearly, I believed him. In my eyes, he loved me, and he would not lie to me. I was naïve. Even if the signs were staring me in the face I managed to convince myself that he would be my husband one day. The clothing I found in his closet was not for his nephew - it was for his son. The second child he had with his wife. Our child was his third. At this point in the game, all my doors were closed. My decision to raise my baby on my own was a direct refusal to settle for a married man who was a pathological liar.

While I worked and took care of my child, I also worked on my faith in Jehovah and creating a life here in the U.S. My daughter and I attended church weekly. When I could, I supported my mom as well. It didn't matter how shabby our relationship was. I remembered the good and the bad, and I decided to do the Christian thing. After all, she wasn't all evil. She did help me get my high school diploma and made sure I survived. In reality, we were both trying to please Jehovah and forgiveness is key in our walk of life. Throughout those trying years, there were times when I faced unemployment, having no babysitter, and there were even times I had to quit my job in order to take care of KayKay. My two child support cases posed nothing but headaches and disappointments. I closed the first case in order to give R-Jay a fresh start, since his driver's license was suspended as a result of the case. He was a truck driver and couldn't work. He promised to do better. That, too, didn't work, and I finally gave up asking nicely. I opened a second case, refusing to close it, just to teach him a lesson. I do recall him asking why not ask Jesus to help, since he paid the price. He also told me I was a strong woman - he had faith I could handle my issues. He really did not care if his child was ok.

One day, his new mistress cursed me out in family court as I fought for child support. Isn't it amazing how women support a loser and the abuser of another female? Thankfully, I overcame that too. Years went by and KayKay grew into a beautiful child. She excelled in everything she did. We attended church together faithfully and made the best of our lives. I can't say it was easy, but I wanted to be the best mom for her. She didn't ask to be here, but she deserved it. It was one of the reasons I decided to go back to school.

I received my Bachelor's in Business Administration and currently live in Brooklyn, East New York. I reminisce on my life and I realize that everything I had to face helped to complete a large puzzle. I needed each piece to get the total picture. Back in 2005, I became a naturalized citizen. I proudly used this opportunity to carry my daddy's name as well as the name my mom gave me from her husband, which is why I carry two last names. Seventeen years of my existence was attached to Mr. Paton when Mr. Bacchus was my biological dad. Most people think I'm married, but not yet. I'm still open-minded. My struggles made me stronger, and my disappointments gave me a reason to fight back. Although my lifestyle was average and filled with cracks and broken pieces, I never lost hope - hope for change and an end to my cycle of negativity.

3. Sister, Sister

Victoria Regia lily: Guyana National Flower

In 1995, my dad, his wife, and I took a trip to Guyana so that I could be introduced to his side of the family. This is when I met my new sister. To be honest, I felt like this new person I was about to meet would replace the sister I lost. It was somewhat an exciting time in my life.

Living in the U.S. with my dad and his wife wasn't so bad. We'd become well acquainted and he wanted me to meet the rest of my family. This planned vacation to my original homeland was very important so I could meet everyone. That particular year had already been a pretty busy one for me, and it played a role in shaping my life. I didn't meet my mom until I was seven years old, and it wasn't until I was seventeen that I found out my godfather was actually my dad. Initially, my grandmother and siblings were the only family I'd ever known. Many years before my mom took me and my sibling to

Trinidad, my real dad had migrated to America. Over the seventeen years, he looked for me.

However, it was a sticky situation and unfortunately, I wasn't made aware of these issues until I was in my teenage years. Mother was a beautiful person. She was selfless, loved people on purpose, and was always ready to serve. However, she was also too young for marriage, and being in a committed, lifelong relationship at fifteen years old, she was destined to make some mistakes. This is why I determined that I was, for lack of better words, a mistake. This same year, I met my biological sister, Ally. She was five years younger than me, and she was a beautiful girl. Things were completely different in my homeland, however.

I had a great time with family, and I was even introduced to a guy. His name was Sammy, and he was also Indian. My grandma had picked him for me to marry, so the trip was also meant for me to meet him, though my dad did not know about Sammy. He was a goldsmith, and made me a ring and a chain. We hung out for the week while I was in Guyana, but I felt rejected by some of his family members, so I decided to move on. They didn't like the idea of us being together. However, my new sister and I bonded a bit and we confided in each other. I told Ally about the arrangement, and we started to build a bond. However, for years, Ally's mother controlled her.

My sister's mother blocked all the visa applications Ally sent out and kept my sister from coming to the U.S. In fact, our dad tried to steal her passport and apply for her visa on his own, but since Ally's mom controlled the entire situation, it did not work. She then promised my dad he would never get his child to leave the country because of what she told the embassy employees.

After fifteen years passed, and Ally's mother had died, Ally asked our dad to prepare her visa application. Father began the process and we were all excited as we waited for the U.S. Embassy to get back to us.

At this time, Ally had two children of her own – Mickey and Bunny. Once the blood test came back, our goal was to add Ally's kids to the visa application. My father's name was placed on Ally's birth certificate, but he never signed it. Her mom used a deed poll process to legally add the family name, Bacchus, as Ally's name. Therefore, a DNA test was needed to confirm he was indeed her father. Sadly, the process came to an end very quickly; she was not my sister because she was not my dad's biological child. Talk about crushed! Her mother was now dead and no one knew who her actual father was. She was the only sister I had left because Natty was also not my sister. However, in my heart, they are still both family. In the meantime, Ally's dreams of coming to America were crumbled, as she received the shock of her life. The choices we make can hurt our loved ones.

Her mother had lied to my dad for so many years. We all thought she was telling the truth until the DNA test proved otherwise. Although we are not sisters, we shared the same disappointment of being lied to. My mother lied to hide her shame while Ally's mom lied for her own security. Thank God, we still have each other. The visa and DNA incident happened in 2010. In March 2015, my dad had a stroke. I took care of him during that time and in 2017, I took a vacation to visit Guyana.

While there, I spoke to a lawyer and completed the process for Ally to get a ten-year visa. Since my dad was unable to visit her, I wanted them to spend some time together. When she came to the U.S., she lived with us for six months. During her time with us, we took another DNA test only to confirm that the first one was correct. However, she completed her stay and then returned home. As normal, we had some fun times and we did bump heads. Our relationship was new, so it wasn't like it was unexpected.

When I think how I lost two women who I thought were my sisters, it still breaks my heart. Natty and I started out as sisters who shared the same father. We all believed we had the same dad. The truth surfaced, leaving my two brothers as half-siblings and Natty became just the person I remembered as my little sissy.

Now, this new sister was also taken away from me in a sense. At this time, I hadn't seen or communicated with Natty for over thirty years. After I had migrated to Trinidad, I was told she had also migrated to another country. I knew the day would come when we would met again and I would explain everything. One day, on Facebook, she found me in a group for all things Guyanese. We were both excited to see each other on social media and shortly after, I had to let her know the truth. After so many years of not seeing each other, I was about to share some bad news: we did not share the same dad. Of course, she had another mother, but for years, in our minds, we had the same father.

I thought about her for many years, hoping we'd meet one day. Here we were, talking on Facebook, and I had to reveal this devastating news. Natty lived on another Caribbean island for some time before moving to London. When we reconnected, she was living in the U.K. Ally always lived in Guyana and she never left until 2017 when she came to see us in New York. I'm grateful for my life. Everyone has a story to tell, and this is mine.

4. Reflections

Trinidad Double Guitar Steelpan - the type of instrument I played.

As I reminisce on my childhood days, my mind captures the good and bad I endured. There was a cemetery in my neighborhood where I visited each day only to see strangers weep for their loved ones. This cemetery provided our main source of water. It's what we called the "standpipe" in my village. Everyone came to fetch water, wash clothes, and even bathe. Most of the villagers didn't have flowing water in their homes, so this was a free and clean alternative. We were squatters. Our lives were different.

My brothers would carry buckets of water to fill up a 500-gallon tank so we could have enough to wash dishes and do our daily chores. Sometimes, the rain became our savior. We also depended on rainwater that was filtered from the roof. My uncle created a homemade filter with white plastic pipes and some mesh. The water was sifted through this setup and we'd boiled it before drinking. We had a gas tank stove for cooking. My mom used to hook a green rubber tube from the top of the tank to the back of the stove.

We were able to do basic cooking and baking, so even though it wasn't a fancy updated appliance, we were happy. Moving from Guyana to Trinidad back in 1982 did bring about some challenges. My grandma's living conditions were much more suitable, so we never had to live without electricity. Squatters didn't get free land and the basic things in life. Technically, we were living on stolen land.

My mom as a single parent did her best for us. She was a great cook, an evangelist, and a good mother. She loved me on many days, and with the same breath, she popped me with a belt, guava whip, or even sent pot covers across the room when she felt I needed discipline. I didn't know it back then, but this was abuse, and most families made us believe this was normal.

Corporal punishment made me angry and depressed. Left undiagnosed, I only got more beatings. On April 9, 2014, my mother died six days after her sixty-third birthday. I wished we had more time together. As I grew older, I realized more and more that she was a good woman and all that she did was for us and God. She wanted us to do right but her approach was wrong. After describing her ugly side, many might say this does not define a person being good. Sometimes, we have to see people's weakness and not label them. In the Bible, the term "Generational Curses" is discussed. In ignorance, she did what she knew. She did not break the cycle, but finding the love of God does help to shape a person's behavior.

She was an awesome pastor. After many years of being an evangelist, she became ordained and had a small church. She was my superwoman and a chatterbox. Sometimes, I didn't want to hear her talk, and now I wished she was here to sing and pray with me. She was filled with love, and I think she equally shared that much passion for anger. Getting her angry would bring out another human being.

I personally believe prayer is a great tool, but I don't believe it's the final answer for many of us. Seeking professional help is also okay, but many of us live in denial. Mother could have used some anger management therapy. However, she only chose prayer as her way to cope with her anger. These are the people who hurt the most. Many will take advantage of them. Her love for people wasn't crushed by her flaws. She continued to show love in the midst of her personal struggles. Jehovah saw it fit to take her home. May she rest in peace until we meet again.

"You are blessed. I tried aborting you and it didn't work," are a few words that play a negative role in my mind. Mother uttered these words to me one day, believing she was consoling me. I was shocked and as normal, I swept things under the rug when it hurt me. I so hated the fact that my life mimicked my mom's life. One day in anger, I blurted out at KayKay, "I should have aborted you when I had the chance."I now know this was depression and low self-esteem talking. Her dad asked me to have an abortion back in 1997 and I refused. Sometimes, I'm at a breaking point and I become overwhelmed. Mother probably had those days, too, so I decided to end this pattern of behavior. I'm glad I learned how to break the cycle. As a mom, I found other ways to teach my child. KayKay is now twenty-one and she is a classy and calm character who is a force to be reckoned with.

I also remember being sexually assaulted when I was thirteen years old. I was flashed by a group of strangers that same year.

When I was young, I had really long hair. My mom didn't know how to comb it well, so I would visit a lady named Patsy who would comb it for me.

One day, as I left her house and began walking home, a group of teenage boys stopped me and decided to take advantage of me. I yelled and fought them off as they grabbed and touched me. It was only God who saved me. I think they felt sorry for me as I cried, so they decided to stop. As soon as I got the chance to run, I ran home and told everyone.

My uncle and brothers searched for them, but they were unsuccessful. It turned out the boys didn't live in my neighborhood, so no one knew them.

I also encountered sexual abuse for a period of time at home. I lied to my mom when she suspected this and to this day, I never told anyone. Since confessing is a form of healing, I'm choosing to share this now.

Both of my siblings are older than I am and I looked up to them for protection, No matter what, I expected them to be there for me. When Gavin tried to penetrate me, I was surprised, confused, and, in my mind, he would not hurt me. He is my big brother. I didn't understand why and what he was doing to me. He asked me to stay quiet, so I did. Mother came home while he was still in the process and she suspected it. I was scared. I knew it was something wrong since I heard it in her voice, so I lied. She asked me over and over again and I continued to lie. In a strange way, my brother and I became closer after the incident. It was almost like a form of repentance. We never spoke of it again. I buried this incident so far in my mind, it became a vague memory. One day, when I was having an argument with Bryant, he threw it in my face. He was aware of what was happening and didn't step in. This was a shock, but Mother had since died so at that point, I had no one to talk to. I actually confronted him since I wrote this book. He did it to two more family members. Initially He was in complete denial and accused us of ganging up against him. After a few months , he dismissed my claim since it was only once. He said my cousin was promiscuous and would blame any man for abusing her. Then one of my niece apparently needed a Gyn and as a good uncle he inspected her once. Currently I am not talking to him it has been over 1 year , I refuse to let him near my heart. I truly believe we can love and forgive people and keep them out of or circle.

This book reflects my true struggles, and my decisions that caused my rebelliousness to God. I learned that honesty is the best policy. My goal is not to project a perfect image, but to show my flaws as a woman and a child of God. Even though I am Christian, in the Bible Paul the apostle confess of having real struggles. Romans 7:23 tells us there is a war between the law of the mind and the law of sin. Paul continues to write in Romans 7:15, that we do not understand why we do the things we're not supposed to do even though we meant to do better. It's like an inner battle we face in life as we struggle with being human and being spiritual.

I can say in my walk It's hard being faithful to God, but with his help all things are possible. When I was 24 years old I had an abortion and I promised myself to take this secret to my grave. NO ONE knows about this part of my life. I felt compelled to share because it can help other women.

In fact This is a major issue in our society today. Is abortion right No!

However as humans we have the right to be wrong this is the reason Jesus died Yes God forgives!

Some might say, isn't it hypocritical to be a Christian, to be against abortion, and yet to actually commit the act in my past history.

Let me explain, being a young mom and unmarried, it was a bad decision to have a second child. I also know the choice I made back then, was not something I wanted to repeat. This is when I made the decision to go Celibate and I lasted for 10 years. In my 35th year I backslide from my church life. I was angry with God for not blessing me with a husband.

I now know he was looking out for me, I needed growth in order to be a wife and I still do. I probably would've been divorced by now if I had it my way. I'm so Glad that God sees everything and he won't put more on us than we can carry.

Women please appreciate being single, know that marriage is not the answer for everyone. Many of us just need to find a relationship with ourselves and most of all with God. Don't let anyone rush you into misery, Give The most High the opportunity to work on YOU.

Hey listen up, having an abortion is not the end of the world. It simply means you have to pick up the pieces and make CHANGES. On the flip side having my baby girl is also not the end of the world, this allowed God to have his way in my life. Trust me they were days I wanted to give up and this same unplanned pregnancy was the reason I held on. Remember ALL THINGS work together for our Good Romans 8:28.

God could change anyone and he forgives, the goal is not to abuse his grace by repeating our actions. After all my doings, a baby out of wedlock, an abortion, faithfulness for many years then backsliding and falling away from the church. He still loves me and I'm still excited about that. I'm taking this time to live for him and to reconcile our relationship. Maybe one day he'll bless me with marriage, in the meantime I'm living to live again- The Promise Land.

One year, I dated a young man named Kaymar Carrington. Kaymar was a tall Jamaican delight who was eight years younger than me. We both had good careers and saw each other nearly every day since we worked in the same building. I was so starved for male companionship, and this relationship was just what I needed. I met Kaymar shortly after my true love died - Walter, AKA Waltz, on November 21, 2010 from respiratory complications.

After Waltz's passing, my life felt severely empty. I needed something to fill that void. Starting over was a form of quenching my thirst for adult company. Waltz, I'm convinced, was my soul mate. In less than one year, he became the person I needed, and for him, I was always willing to go the extra mile. He was also the person I hated since I found out he was cheating. At the beginning of our relationship, he told me he lived with his mom because he recently got laid off. I even visited his home and met this girl named Stacy who was supposedly his mom's friend. She and I spoke, he was ill at the time, so we worked together to encourage him to take his medication. Waltz and I spent mostly evenings together because I worked during the daytime. As the months went by, I realized his phone calls were more and more private and he always had to run. Finally, after I confronted him, he made a partial confession Stacy was his roommate, or at least, so he stated. He initially kept the truth from me because he did not know if I would trust him after learning he had a female roommate.

Well, that was only half of the situation. This roommate turned into a lover and partner in a weed distribution service. They shared the same type of lifestyle, so I was a misfit anyway. I remember him saying to me, "You are the type of woman I want so I can change. You can motivate me."Moving forward, the games continued. To put me at ease, he said she left and moved to Long Island. I even went to his home and spent the whole day. I really believed him. Soon, I learned Stacy never left. She went to her sister's home that day to see her son. For whatever reason, her son did not live with her, so this was Waltz's strategy to get me back in his life. Clearly, I forgave him, only to find out he lied to me again. In fact, his previous roommate was back in his life when we were still dating.

Actually, two days before he died, we broke up and I never got the chance to reconcile. His girlfriend and I traveled in the same car to attend his funeral. I do not have a license, so for me to get to the cemetery would have cost me $100 in cab fares. Her friend Coleen was driving and said, "I know you love him and would want to be there, so you can ride in my car. Stacy will be cool with it." I trusted Coleen and, in fact, it was a way to make peace. Hating would not bring him back. The day he died, Stacy was with him. I felt it in my soul, that day when I was at work. I wanted to call him. Naturally, I pushed this urge to the side because I was still angry with him.

On my way home, I read the words on my Facebook newsfeed: "RIP Waltz. You will be missed." Since we were Facebook friends, Waltz's timeline posts kept coming up in my notifications. I had a difficult time processing this information. His son was his junior and I wasn't sure which Waltz had died. When it became clear, reality set in. He was gone. He left this world before we could talk again. He was with her and not with me. I guess that was meant to be.

Back to Kaymar: he was an active military personnel. A few months had passed since Waltz's death and in March 2011, I met Kaymar. Since he had just returned from his deployment, a committed relationship was not his goal. That, however, was his excuse for not committing to an actual relationship. I just ran with it. I was gullible, needy, and recovering from the unexpected death of my true love. This fruitless relationship went on. Sex became the main attraction as opposed to dating. I guess somewhere in the back of my mind, I was hoping he would change - that he would see and want me for who I was. During our fling, I saw signs, but naturally, I ignored them, as most women do. He spent less and less time with me. It got to the point that our seldom phone calls became our real source of communication.

Meeting up was forced into our busy schedule, but only to satisfy our sexual drive. One day, I realized that going to Florida was a regular trip for Kaymar. When confronted, he snapped and profusely denied my assumptions. After asking why he made several trips to Florida and if he was seeing someone over there, he said he was visiting his needy sister. She had three children and needed his help. I believed him and left it alone. Life continued and so did our friendship. We were becoming buddies, which I enjoyed. After all, I wanted to be included in his life. Even though there was no real commitment, having someone to talk to made me feel important and, in a weird way, it made me feel loved.

His explanation about Florida, however, was not enough to convince me he was sincere. It was always an issue, so I left room for disappointment just in case I was not the only one. A part of me still wanted more. I wanted an exclusive relationship with no doubt in my mind that he was honest. After over one year, my conclusion was not surprising. I knew I was taking a chance, but I took the steps anyway. Finally, I convinced myself that what Kaymar and I had was actually a game. I became desperate after the loss of my true love, and I really expected too much from this relationship Kaymar and I shared. I made it clear that we were not a good fit, but we still stayed in contact via phone.

In December 2012, I met someone new. He wanted the same things I wanted. Never in my life had I dated so many guys in such a short time. In fact, after breaking up with the father of my child, I was single for over ten years. I guess now, I was on a roll to catch up on all the time I felt I had lost. Kaymar, on the other hand, wanted only my body, so my poor mindset pushed me into another error. Looking for love in all the wrong places is the best way to put it. Starting over was definitely an option. I decided to give this new person a shot and hoped for the best. Maybe he would finally be the one.

In reality, I was a pastor`s daughter, born and raised in the church, living a backslidden life, and my choices were poor. Looking for love was my main focus and making mistake after mistake was my new way of living. Starting over seemed like an awesome idea, and for once, I felt I was old enough to know what was best for me. My new boyfriend's name was Ronald Wilson. He wasn't the picture I wanted, but he was workable. I lived long enough to know that sometimes, good things come in disguise. Plus, he wasn't ugly, but he was okay. Ronald didn't have a job, but he had plans – good plans, and they sparked my attention. However, he was a felon, acquitted after waiting on trial for twenty months. According to the report, he was accused of stealing a cop's gun from the 103rd precinct when they were doing a cash-for-guns buy-back trade. After learning he was found not guilty, I decided to give him a chance and not judge him based on his past.

Now that he was given another shot at life and he was willing to start over with me, I was willing to help him. We quickly began our friendship and I took the opportunity to let Kaymar know that, since we were going in separate directions, our little friendship was coming to an end. I still wanted to be some type of friends with him, though, which made Ronald angry. At that time, I was unable to see Ronald's controlling ways, but later on, it became clearer.

My new relationship was off to a bumpy start, but moving forward felt like my only option I had, so I continued. It was clear to me that I was wrong to jump from one guy to the next that quickly. My entire mindset was in the wrong place and my life was spinning out of control. During my dating period, Ronald's behavior became alarming when he actually got jealous of my dead boyfriend. Waltz was deceased for two years, but in eight months, he left an impression in my heart. I guess the fact that I never got to say goodbye and I didn't get a chance to reconcile haunted me for months. In my anger, I actually told Waltz I hoped he would die, not knowing he would die two days later. Even apologizing for some of the horrible things I said in our last argument was not possible, so my healing process was not smooth. Ronald wanted me to remove all of Waltz's pictures from my Facebook. A few pieces of his clothing were still at my home, so Ronald made me throw them away. He forced me to heal when I wasn't ready to let go of this pain I carried for two years.

Ronald also wanted me to cease all communications with Kaymar since he saw him as a threat. He didn't want to talk about his past that much, hence why I did not know the rest of his rich history with NYPD until later on in the relationship.

We had a few disputes that almost became violent. In fact, one time, he snatched my phone and pushed me on the bed. I accepted all this since I was blinded by my desire to make it work. This time, I was determined to do whatever it takes to keep someone in my life. I was wrong, but seeing this at that time was not an easy thing to do. I guess I just kept an open mind, hoping everything would work itself out in the end. One day, I took my daughter out to lunch and Ronald came along with us. Prior to dating him, I had never let a guy close to my child. Kaymar and I met at his home and Waltz and I mainly hung out in the evening when Kaykay was asleep. She was sixteen years old at the time, so I no longer thought it was a problem.

She was no longer a toddler and was capable of speaking up if she needed to. Some might say three months is too soon to introduce a new guy to her, but my child wasn't the average teenager. I recall one day, he stuck his head in her room to say hello. At that time, she was with her cousin while they were doing their homework. She quickly advised him to never enter her room or even look inside. Ronald was angry and kept complaining about it, but I told him she was right, and her room was off-limits.

Now back to the lunch date. He did not pay - I did. He was working at that time, but wasn't making much, so I volunteered to pay most of the time. While we were dining, I was trying to get my kid to eat chicken. My daughter is a red meat person, so that didn't work well. I backed off and allowed her to eat what she wanted. On my way home, everything was fine. However, when he had the chance, Ronald mentioned the room and the chicken versus beef issues. He deemed me to be an unfit mother because I didn't assume my parenting roles, expecting me to punish or discipline my child right there as we were dining.

He and I argued and he left. I really didn't care because at this point, I had had enough of Ronald's behavior. Shortly after, I called one of my girlfriends who advised me to do a background check using an App which I recommend every female do before dating someone new. I went through the process and found out the entire three-month relationship was all a lie. We were now facing a breakup because building another relationship based on lies and deception was not my goal. Ronald actually had an insanely long rap sheet – so, he came with more issues than I thought.

Being falsely accused by the NYPD for the buy-back gun charge was the least of his problems. That time, he may have been innocent, but several times before, he was certainly guilty and he kept all of it a secret. He was charged with posing as a fireman, bank fraud, and stealing his father's gun to be a cop for one day. He was known to be a serial impersonator to the media.

By this time, I had gathered all the information I needed and I eased my way out of the relationship. I was now being accused of cheating.

Ronald said Kaymar and I were still in a relationship and this was the real reason why I didn't want to be with him anymore. In actuality, I was afraid of the man I thought I knew.

The possibility of having a stable relationship quickly became a nightmare. However, Ronald didn't see it that way. In his bizarre mind, I had issues with being faithful. At the time, I was working for the TSA, so I felt the need to keep a low profile. I told Ronald it was best for us to take a break, and that maybe if it's meant to be, God would work it out. Knowing very well I had no intention of giving him another chance, I asked him to give me some space. Sadly, in his head, taking a break meant showing up to my job completely unannounced. Ronald became openly over-possessive, verbally abusive, and psychotic.

He began stalking me and sending death threats via email and text message. He hacked my Facebook, GMail, and AOL accounts with the intention of making my life miserable. He even created a blog with my name and stole pictures from my Facebook page. People who saw were contacting me on Facebook. He stated I had HIV and was infecting coworkers, and accused me of being a child abuser. In fact, I had several cases opened since he made a few 911 calls, lying that he witnessed me hitting my child with a 2-by-4 in her stomach. The fake story he created and shared, as well as these calls, had little effect on my job. However, it took a great toll on my sleep and overall health.

After contacting some online bullying services and reporting my case to Facebook, the articles and blogs came down. Apparently, he had purchased a wedding ring after less than six months of dating. Amusingly, it was from a pawn shop. To be honest, I would have never worn the ring. I never saw it, but the idea of getting my dream ring from a pawn shop was not my goal. Thank God he never showed it to me. But his only friend, Marcus, told me about it through Facebook Messenger. To this day, I never found out if his one friend was real or imaginary. Marcus assured me that I was in trouble since I decided to stop dating Ronald.

Even the person who I spoke to at the Queens District office wasn't sure if this accomplice was an actual human being. They never told me if they found out, but they helped me. During this ordeal, I learned that I shared the same last name as Ronald's ex-wife. Thankfully, she'd escaped the madness. We were not related, but coincidentally, his ex-wife`s sister and my cousin had the same name - Melissa. His stepson and my nephew also had the same name - Shaquille. When reality set in, at one point in time, we even lived two blocks away from each other.

So, it was my conclusion that this man did his homework when he was released from jail. Maybe he was looking for his ex-wife and found me. The Queens D.A. did confirm Ronald had a short history of threatening and stalking a few people from his ex-relationships. He became a real nightmare. He also terrorized me by swearing he would get his friends from the past to kill Kaymar. This made me worried. I felt responsible, so I kept contacting Kaymar to warn him. Despite my good intentions, this made Kaymar angry. He warned me to stop reaching out to him since he wasn't afraid of my boyfriend.

Kaymar's new wife, AKA his "sister" who lives in Florida, was not happy with me contacting him. The "sister" who had three children and needed help took it upon herself to shut me down and insult me. It's amazing how women will defend a deadbeat man and trample another woman who they've never met. Her name was Chanice

Kingston, a Jamaican chick, so they were both Jamaican. I guess I would have never been good enough for him anyway.

I had no idea who she was and I think she could say the same for me since we never actually met. However, I knew Chanice was the mysterious sister Kaymar kept visiting in Florida. He played me well and the pain felt less severe knowing I was the one who dumped him for my new boo. The only thing was, this new boo was a nut case. It felt like I didn't even win. I still lost and life was dishing me some new pains. In essence, Kaymar had a fun time having two women in two separate states. How easy it was for him. But I had no time to sit around feeling sorry for myself.

I was too busy trying to cope with sleepless nights and other terrors from Ronald Wilson, who seemed to be enjoying the way he tormented me. As my dilemma continued, I was in for many more surprises. Ronald and I broke it off in March 2013. He was actually arrested in February 2014, so he had a fun time stalking me for nearly one year. By that time, I'd learned he had accessed my Social Security number, my daughter's Social Security, and my New York State ID number. Now that he had these personal pieces of information, he swore my life would be a living hell. He even went as far as to email me death threats from fake Yahoo accounts.

Life certainly took a lash at me. I was hit really hard, but I managed to summon the strength I needed to move on. I got a restraining order and Jehovah provided a way to get Ronald off the streets for two years as he sat in jail awaiting trial. Once out of jail, he placed fifty fake phone calls from his cell phone to 911. He claimed an officer was shot, but after being tricked a few times, NYPD got him and locked him up. In 2016, he was sentenced to six years total, with a 2020 release date.

With spiritual and mental therapy, I was able to overcome the pain from the experience. Prayer does change things and my therapist, Joe, played a great role in my healing process. I'm forever grateful for the time he invested in me. I am now moving on with wounded wings and choosing to remain optimistic. Broken relationships are a recipe for failure, and not healing after a breakup is just another disaster waiting to happen. It was really traumatizing losing one boyfriend who died suddenly, especially knowing he died two days after our big argument. I never got to say sorry, never got to make up or make peace before his departure, and even now, it still hurts.

To make matters worse, Ronald tried forcing me to heal and to move on by destroying what few tangible memories I had. I could never replace them, but good people will always live on in our souls. Walter had issues like every one of us, but he was an awesome friend. Choosing to settle also helped to create my catastrophes. I could truly say I went from bad to worst. Kaymar was bad, but Ronald was a total disaster. I am now convinced that I never really healed and I kept moving on. It's such a common act but this time, it's my story. Having these experiences truly helped to mold me and it pushed me back to basics.

For a short period, I turned away from my faith. Things were not working out the way I wanted, so I tried to fix it myself. It's just another part of life, some may say, but having firsthand experiences weighs more, as opposed to hearing someone else's story. I still believe we can avoid these issues if we listen to others. My life is not a walk in the park, but it's a roller coaster that I would not exchange. It has truly made me who I am today.

I must also make it clear that my teenage daughter never liked Ronald. She thought he was weird and untrustworthy. It's amazing how our children can see clearer than us when it comes to making judgments of character. It was time to take a break. I needed to take time to recuperate.

6. Emotions and Betrayal

Sometimes, we fight fire with fire, and it makes things worst. When betrayal meets betrayal, the pain becomes inevitable.

My mom was a pastor. She raised me to believe in Jehovah. When I was a child, she was an evangelist, and we visited several churches before we finally settled at the COGIC denomination.

For about a year during our search, we were members of a Spiritual Baptist Church. This was a disaster. I was always scared during services. They would ring a bell and throw raw rice at church members.

The bell represented the voice of God calling them. They answered

Him by ringing the bell. Rice was a sign of prosperity, so they spread that throughout the church. I'm not sure where in the Bible Jesus did this, process of fasting and praying in a room for several days. You cannot leave to go home. For a specific time, the person would be attended to and they would remain at the church until the mourning is completed. Only when you are eighteen or older were you were allowed to do this, so my prayer was to be out of the church by that age. This strange procedure was scary. The mother of the church, who is seen as the leader, or the equivalent of the First Lady in the U.S.A., would take white chalk and draw a box. The person who was mourning would lay down inside. This act represented burying the person so they could rise up in the newness of Christ.

I always ask my mom, if Christ already walked out of the tomb, why should I go back in? She told me to be quiet, so I just followed her faithfully. They had volunteers called spiritual nurses who would attend to your needs, such as performing mini baths, keeping candles lit, and offering liquids to drink. Being I was still a child, the scariest part for me was the act of placing a cloth or bandana-type bandage over the eyes. Seeing was a form of distraction, so blocking out all vision would allow the mourners to focus more on praying and seeking God.

I thank the Lord each day that He allowed my mom to leave that church just in time for my eighteenth birthday. I never mourned at that church, but I was baptized at that crazy place. At the tender age of fifteen, I could remember my hands burning as the wax fell from the candle I was holding all night. These acts represented Jesus, who is the light of the world. This church did extra steps. Nowhere in the Bible did anyone hold a candle to represent Jesus, but they felt it was necessary.

Later on that night, during my baptism, I almost drowned as they dipped me three times in the river. At the second dip, I slipped out of the minister's hands. That was not such a good experience, so my first baptism was a mess. To make matters worse, months later, we learned that the man who baptized me was not married, but had a lady with three children out of wedlock. A functioning fornicator cannot knowingly hold a position as a Christian leader. We all struggle, but being honest is important, especially when we know better. He had no business baptizing anyone. In fact, he was supposed to be in Bible class learning how to overcome his struggles. As the years went by, Mother and I learned a lot of hidden secrets they held in that church, so finally, we left and settled in the COGIC ministry where I had my second baptism.

I was still in high school when all of this happened. Although I was baptized, my mom allowed me to be a member of my high school steel band group.. Most People who are into the church are not too keen on carnival activities. Anything that is associated with Parties, Parades or bacchanal is frowned upon by the church. However I am glad my mom allowed me to take part in my High School band. I met a lot of nice people and one of them was Legendary. His father was our instructor.

Mr. G. was introduced to us and I never forgot him. He was a quiet and laid-back person who always greeted you with a smile. A few years later, he died, leaving his son, Legendary, to carry on his legacy. My brother became close with his family, so we all stayed in touch as much as possible. Years later, I ran into Legendary in Brooklyn. It was one of those amazing coincidences because we were both living separate lives.

One day, he came to my home with his girl looking for my eldest brother. After talking for a bit, he left and I didn't see him again for many years. Later, I found out he'd gotten in trouble with the law. Mommy was the one who'd kept in touch with him. That woman was like a piece of glue. She always kept things together and showed love. She cared a lot about people and she was concerned about Legendary's twenty-five-year sentence.

According to what I know now, he had multiple charges, including 2nd degree murder. It did not matter that he was not the only one involved or even the fact that he wasn't guilty of everything he was charged with. The law of the streets says no snitching, so he protected his family by taking the time and no plea bargain.

While he was incarcerated, Legendary tried to stay in touch, but unfortunately, he was moved around a bit and Mom lost track of him. A few years later, she died, but she didn't leave before mentioning him to us. Two years after her death, while cleaning out my basement, I found a little book that belonged to her. In it, she had information concerning Legendary, our little star player, who everyone knew as being a great steel pan student. He learned the skill well and he was also taught by his dad Mr G. Fast-forward, He was still incarcerated at that time, and after a moment of contemplation, I took it upon myself to search for him.

In 2016, I found him. He was in solitary confinement for a violent act, which he claimed was necessary to survive. He convinced me that everyone left him for dead and he had no more support from his family, his baby mothers, or anyone else. We reconnected and built a friendship, which led to a long-distance relationship. When a woman has been through multiple failed relationships, she tends to continuously self-sabotage. In my case, it was no different, and I was now building a relationship with a prisoner who needed me for financial and emotional support. I needed him to fill a gap of loneliness, which I didn't realize back then.

After two years of a testing battle, I decided to give up on my dreams of becoming his wife. He had asked me to marry him while he was in prison. I knew he was desperate at the moment because we were having a heated argument, so I didn't buy it. This was not how I dreamed I would get married, so I told him we should wait. It was best to take our time since I didn't believe in divorce. I had already met his family and we built a connection, so I allowed them to enter my world. To be honest, half of what they were saying about him eventually came to light. His family warned me of his selfish ways. He was not satisfied most times. He could get demanding sometimes. I soon found that they were right.

However, since he'd already broken it off with his baby mother, I was now his queen. Kris, his child's mother, also tried to warn me. She told me since I had a job and he was in jail, I would be the one he needs to get by but again, I didn't listen. I felt like both she and his family were wrong. He had me brainwashed into believing and trusting him completely. I was blinded until he asked me to do some illegal activity like providing contraband. I was the person he pushed to call all his friends and family to ask them for money when I didn't have any more to give. This man was never satisfied - he always wanted more.

I'm not sure what he was doing in prison, but he claimed he needed extra money to buy food. I sent money for him, and his mom did as well. Sometimes, he said his life was in danger and he needed money to avoid the gangs. This was not true. It was a form of extortion. Once I finally realized what was happening, I decided to confront him about me not being able to afford to send him any more money. After all, I lived in New York City and had a college kid, so it was really expensive. This is when he came up with a bright idea for me to conduct illegal activities, which if I'm being honest, I actually thought about for some time. However, I eventually declined to provide any contraband.

When you love someone more than you love yourself, it's a recipe for blindness. One day, I felt like it was time to go, and this wasn't going to work anymore. I expressed that to him as well as his mom. She really didn't give me her opinion, but later on, I learned that she discussed it with him. I chose to walk, but it wasn't what I really wanted. In my mind, he and I still had a chance. He managed to talk me into a comfort zone, where I wasn't really committed yet I wasn't really gone. He said he was embarrassed that I told his family, and he wanted to try and reconcile.

I tried it his way for a while, but when I felt it was too much to handle, I wanted to leave and explore. Unfortunately, I still couldn't move on. This man, who was clearly no good for me, still had me under lock and key. In fact, based on the way he was clinging to me, I felt like we still had a chance. After all, if he loved me the way he said he did, and clearly I'm finding it difficult to move on, maybe Jehovah was showing us we were actually meant for each other.

7. Let's rewind…

Legendary and I both felt like God put us back in each other's lives. I'd known him since he was thirteen and I was sixteen. He was too young at the time and I wasn't really into guys since I was a late bloomer, but I knew I liked him from the first day. Now, in our adulthood, I continued to mentally, morally, and financially assist him, even though I expressed it wouldn't work. Every time he asked me if I had another man, I'd tell him no. And even though it was the truth, since I had already expressed I wanted to move on, he didn't believe me. Frankly, I never changed a thing, so clearly he saw I wasn't going anywhere.

Going back about eight months before, I trusted him so blindly, I allowed him to talk me into reconnecting him to an old friend - a woman. Apparently, they began a relationship behind my back. He loved money so much, now his mom, this new woman, and I were all financially supporting him. Once I got wind of what was really happening, his girlfriend, Alisha, and I had a few choice words. She was overweight. He always assured me that she was not his type and he wasn't attracted to fat girls. Well, that was a lie.

When I suspected this relationship between the two of them was real, I decided to step back. Two months later, when I was vacationing in Trinidad, his two sisters and his mom took me and my niece Alicia to a waterfront park. While we were hanging out, I secretly took pictures of them. This is one of my weaknesses. Trying to get his attention, I even sent these pictures of his family to the cell phone he was using as contraband. My goal was to get his attention, so I desperately used anything I had.

In April 2019, I was feeling extremely depressed and defeated. In a way, I lost him, even though he was still alive. The pain and emptiness felt familiar, like when my mother died in April 2014. I kept texting him and even though I knew he read my messages, he never responded. I was losing all self-worth - this man destroyed me. Alisha and I spoke on the phone. It was April 6, 2019 when I inboxed her on Facebook. This wasn't the first time we spoke, and I wanted to warn her just like Kris warned me, but that didn't go too well. When she read my message, Alisha asked me for my number.

I guess I'm the fool who had her number saved in my phone. Legendary had me calling her to check up on other friends. Either way, I gave her my number so she could call me. I didn't know it then, but she made a three-way call so he was secretly listening to our conversation. This three-way call lasted for a short five minutes. This was when she chose to inform me that he was her man, and he would not be speaking to me because she did not give him permission to do so. She also stated that he had to respect what she said, so he wouldn't be speaking to me anytime soon.

That day, it was made clear that Alisha was only talking to me just to confirm what he said was true so she could make a clearer decision. Wow, talk about me being played. She was being made his new queen. During that five-minute call, for a split second, I lost my sanity, my heart felt like it stopped, and the evil in me came forth. The only tool I had was the very phone I was texting him on - the same one he was using to listen to that call, so I used it to my advantage. I'm the one who caused him to be in confinement, when I called the warden and spoke to him about everything. But I also felt like he had friends in high places so he didn't suffer any real consequences. In reality, he betrayed me by holding onto me as a prop while he double-dipped.

It was when I caught him lying to me that he turned the tables by completing his deceptive move and ostracizing me. However, there was a part of me that wanted him to feel the same pain, so I frantically made this choice to return the betrayal. In the end, what difference would it make if he is sent to the hole for two or three months? This form of punishment would not have any tremendous effect on his current twenty-five-year sentence. Alisha continued texting me since I had already ended the call. This was when I learned Legendary had already taken the liberty to let her know his baby mother and I had a previous conversation back in May 2017.

He twisted the truth and said we had a big argument, which was not true. Kris and I had a respectful and adult conversation concerning him. She even said to me she was happy I was there for him, but he was a liar and I needed to be careful. He knew everything Kris said to me that day.

He had asked me to send him screenshots of our text messages. Here I am, proving that Kris, the mother of his kids, was right - he is a liar. This man connected Alisha and I and made us become Facebook friends. I even became Facebook friends with her sister, DeeDee. When he confirmed his love for Alisha, he completely blacklisted me. I was no longer worthy. I was devalued. I felt scorned and rejected. This mentally broke me down. They had more in common than I thought.

She was into weed smoking, got him a contraband phone and was also a 3rd degree felon. Clearly, they were suitable for each other. I did not want to accept this though.

I was hoping to reconcile. I kept telling myself if he loved me as much as I loved him, he wasn't going anywhere. I was so wrong. He tied me to his side just so he could complete his mission and then proceeded to dash me against the walls. When he said he needed me, the truth was, he actually needed the money I was sending him. He chose to lie to me because he needed a crutch just until he got to the other side. Needless to say, this crushed me.

I lowered my standards to the point where I begged him for another chance. I felt like my heart was being ripped apart. I cried so much and even attempted to hurt myself. I showed him my physical scars, trying to get him to understand how much he destroyed me. Nothing worked. He was gone, and Alisha was laughing at me. She threw things in my face that I had confided in him. She knew my business and she was now his queen, while I was the underdog. Now, I was outside the circle, lost, forgotten, and scared. And even still, I longed for another chance with him. I was so low, I didn't see my worth. Although he was long distance and we never made any physical contact, I didn't want to start over with anyone else.

This was the fourth guy I let near my heart in nine years and everything seemed wrong. How come the prisoner cheating affected me the worst? I wanted to give up on life. I wanted to hate men. I wanted to not trust again since he played me. Not only was he dishonest, I was accepting the fact that I was just a dollar sign to him. From support to pain, I was there for him when he was on his face. Now I needed him and he was not there for me during my mental breakdown. In fact, he became the straw that broke the camel's back.

Clearly, he wasn't in love with me, but he was in love with the help I offered him. Somewhere in our short communication after all this happened, he said when I gave him the silent treatment and I stopped sending money for him, she was there. Basically, this new boo was giving him money and therefore, she was elevated above me. Maybe she was a Band-Aid, or maybe she was truly his new love. I was so confused. I didn't know what to think. When I was in Trinidad, his family even entertained me at their home. This left me wondering if they knew what he was up to.

When I was returning on that JetBlue flight. I was secretly praying the plane would crash. It was the moment right after I realized I had been played. It is still hard to move on. I'm stuck. He won't even talk to me after two letters he wrote to me. In his letters, he blamed me for everything and I accepted the blame in the midst of my confused state of mind. I felt like he demonstrated some narcissistic qualities. Somehow, Legendary did not acknowledge that he lied to me by keeping me close just in case he needed a Plan B.

All this time, I was relying on the idea of us working things out while he was building a future with Alisha. In fact, he would say that I was smart. He laughed out loud as he said, "I didn't know you were going to find out." This man really thought my feelings were a big game. Finally, he said for us to just be friends. Then he had the audacity to keep asking for money as if nothing had ever happened. I made it clear that Alisha was now in my role, so she needed to perform as I did for the last three years. I decided being friends would leave me vulnerable.

I felt like I was an option, that he wanted to have his cake and eat it too.

My mind and my heart were not on the same page. Some days, I was strong enough to say it's over and I was worthy of having better. Then, on other days, I would cry my eyes out and yearn for him to contact me. I had to find a form of comfort by telling myself it was for my own good since Jehovah knows the heart. Maybe he's not the one, and after completing his remaining twelve years, he would have hurt me anyway. Somehow, this self-counseling didn't get me through each day. June 26, 2019. It was the last day I made contact with any one of his people, but I randomly started a battle with Alisha's sister, DeeDee.

That day, I was at work at the MTA and my tears were flowing nonstop. Even the customers were looking at me as if I was crazy. This was a difficult day for me and I wanted to share my misery. What do they say? Misery loves company. I think this was a type of coping mechanism for me. DeeDee wasn't that innocent. She sent me a friend request on Facebook when this was all unraveling. Even though it did not directly pertain to her, I felt as if she was a part of the laughing party. In my mind, I was now a big joke and whoever I could reach was going to share in my misery. She called me and we argued about her sister being the one he chose. I was warned to back off because she knew where I worked and she didn't mind taking a trip to New York City from Florida.

After our Facebook war, DeeDee and I decided to leave each other Unblocked and I was on to my next person. A few days later, I reached out to Legendry's sister who lives in Long Island. She pretended that she didn't know who I was when she responded to a text I sent her. In my text message, I told her, "Family comes first, huh?" So I do understand why I'm experiencing the complete silence. I did call and left messages. It's obvious to me that they were being deceptive as well. What did I get? No response.

Maybe they choose not to get involved but at this point, I didn't care. All I wanted was to be heard and to be understood. Legendary was the only male and the last child for his mom. I was thinking, they were the ones that breastfed and encouraged him to be an ungrateful and abusive man. They didn't care about my side of the story, but they welcomed me when I was sending him money for the last three years. Does that sound familiar? Only if they get what they want, then the love is mutual. Children do exhibit what they have been taught at home. In fact, his mom told me their side of the family did not speak to his uncle's side for over ten years. They felt like only Legendary was punished and it was not fair since he was not the only one involved. This bitterness was created when Legendary became incarcerated. I also felt like this is another example of learned behavior - forgiveness was not a strong point for the family.

It's been two months since and I was going through my phone log. I stumbled upon an old letter I wrote to Legendary back in 2017 - the same month Kris and this stranger spoke to me. Jehovah really took the time to protect me, but most times, we don't listen to the voice of The Almighty. Both his baby mother and Angela, who was a stranger, spoke to me in May 2017 about cutting ties. Angela didn't even know me. I wonder what would have happened if I had taken heed. Angela shared her story with me, and explained she was an ex-con and to be careful. I ignored all the warning signs. Maybe this is why I am facing these issues now. She told me about jail talk not being real but desperate pleas. The money, games, and lies are all they plan in the 24 hours they have. After talking to me for about 20 minutes, I learned a lot more about her.

However, she also predicted this very outcome. Angela was like an angel in disguise. At that time back in 2017, I felt like she was a weirdo. She too had a high school sweetheart who was incarcerated and she stood faithful until the end of his jail sentence.

When her sweetheart got home, she learned he had another woman who was visiting him during the fifteen years he was locked up. In the end, his family accepted this other woman and Angela was rejected since she decided to rededicate her life to Christianity. She told me Jehovah had blessed her with the gift of sight just like her grandmother. She also warned me to be a moral support and don't look to Legendary for any type of a relationship. Angela stated, most prisoners don't know what real love is until they come home. "Jail talk" is what they do just so they can receive everything they need to survive that tragedy.

Back in 2017, when I shared this experience with Legendary, he laughed and said he would always love me. He wouldn't ever do anything like that to me. As expected, I fell victim to his lies and buried everything Angela told me. I believed it was just something that happened and it was simply a weird scenario. Fast forward, what she said is all playing out before my eyes. Angela did indeed get some spiritual insight from Jehovah.

I needed a reality check and Sarah Jakes Roberts was my new girl. She was a preacher and I listened to her sermons on repeat. This young lady was helping me get through my pain and rejection. I felt like every time

I stopped the YouTube video, my struggle would come back like a vengeance, but immediately, when I looked at another one of her sermons, my strength would return. I knew I needed to stand on my own, and that's when I decided to pray and read my Bible so Jehovah could bless me with my own strength.

For the last sixty days, I was either writing or reminiscing throughout the day. This overthinking pushed me into depression, so I started seeing a professional. It was the right thing to do since praying alone didn't help me. It's not that Jehovah is not powerful. Sometimes, we need some extra help and it's ok to reach out. I was told by a psychiatrist that my condition presented an emotionally distressed state and I needed medication.

I started taking meds, but I had moments when I relived the pain and cried myself to sleep. Legendary was not the main cause, but surely, he was the culprit to my current health challenge. To combat some of the loneliness, I started doing things with friends. I went out more and started living.

I also reached out to his sister, the one who was a Jehovah's Witness, and she offered me spiritual support. In reality, nothing helped. My heart wasn't healed and I still wanted him. I was convinced I was brainwashed. Clearly, he didn't want me unless I remained the same and did all the things he wanted me to do. Obviously, since I refused to be used, this caused me to totally lose him. But Sarah Jakes said, "When we start creating boundaries, we tend to lose friends." Clearly, this was the case I was now facing.

After no contact for three weeks, I sent him a letter and so regret that. I started praying and crying over the situation again. It was like this act of reaching out opened my wound again. I promised myself I'd stop and never approach his sister again with this situation.

She had been kind and I wanted our connections to continue. She and I were sharing Bible talks. It was helpful to me in general. In reality, I still wanted Legendary. I was in love with a selfish and desperate man who loved money more than life. It's like I was addicted to the abuse, and being hurt was my familiar place. After all, I had a trend of being rejected and hurt for the past eight to nine years. When I further examined my behavior, it was like I was co-dependent. I wanted him to love me when I was supposed to love myself.

It's crazy how I felt like he's not such a bad person. There was some good in him. I'm trying to reason with, and blame myself for some of this. Maybe his prison situation is forcing him to be who he's become. Prison is an ugly thing, and maybe his true personality is not what I'm seeing. Part of me wants to convince myself that I pushed love away since being loved by a man was not my norm. But is this love?

I was so confused and the pain was real. Even if this is not true, and it wasn't my fault, every strong woman will learn and grow from life experiences. If I never had a struggle, I wouldn't have a testimony. The process includes pain and we cannot avoid this type of battle in our lives. I also did and said some things that were ugly when I was in that dark place, so I also hurt him. Hurt people hurt people. His family disappeared too. Family first. I guess it's ok to have a bond. I just wonder if they can stand before The Almighty and defend him one day.

Legendary never contacted me again so the proof is in the pudding - no money, no love. It's obvious he cannot love. He cannot grasp the concept of loving and caring for someone based on his circumstances. Back in 2016 when I reconnected with him, he was in a place of pure desperation. Solitary confinement was no place for him to actually make a clear or fair decision. Even when he came out of confinement, he was desperate, since he claimed that everyone left him for dead. I was wrong to trust him. He wasn't strong enough to even believe in himself, so how could I believe that he really loved me?

Prison is a horrible place and it destroys a human being. It's supposed to reform them, but unfortunately, many of them get worst. Legendary took me off his visitation list way before I caught him creeping. He kept me tied to my dreams only to use me, and he pretended that he needed me when I was ready to walk away. Then, he dumped me when I needed him the most. Think about it - I was there for him when he was on his face, but he was incapable of being there for me!

We all know physically, it wasn't possible for him to be there since he was confined, but I emotionally deceived myself by accepting and believing his fake love was strong. At the time, I was struggling. My father was disabled, having survived a stroke, and my stepmother was on a breathing machine due to her own health issues. I also had other family issues to handle. While I was trying to hold it together, I was also battling insomnia and being borderline diabetic. So my plate was always filled. Yet, Legendary seemed to always demand more. It was never enough for him.

I managed to convince myself neither one of us was strong enough for loving the right way, but I was fair-minded and he was not. Most women would not tell him they wanted to date and move on. I did because I'm generally an honest person. I never practiced lying to anyone. So he was able to make his decisions. Meanwhile, I was hooked until everything was ready to go on his side. When he was ready to make it clear and move on with Alisha, he was playing the victim asking me for my blessings.

Blessings! This let me know they were getting married. Obviously, that was her dream to marry a prisoner in a small room with no real support. There was a part of me that felt sorry for her because it seemed as if they were both desperate and deserved each other. In one of the text messages, she told me she felt sorry for me. I guess her prison marriage would leave me dead!

I'm not sure how much time Alisha served, but the app Been Verified didn't provide much information. Maybe they were a match made in heaven. Then there was another part of me that wished Legendary was in a position to marry me, but only if he was free. Day after day, I kept hitting repeat in my mind. No matter how hard I tried to train my mind to think positive thoughts, somehow I found myself back to that place of darkness.

Wishing him God's blessings then at the same moment, I wished the hand of Jehovah would take vengeance on those who had come against me. It was crazy how I allowed this situation to take me through this emotional roller coaster. I was so miserable that I kept reaching out, hoping to find closure, if only Legendary would admit his flaws, but that wasn't possible. Moving on, wounded, was my only option.

Once again, I reached out for male companionship. I confided in a male coworker who seemed to be interested in my wellbeing. But soon, I found that his intentions were not pure. Thank God, I was conscious enough to run away from this trap. Ladies - be careful who you let in your circle. This could have been another failed relationship, sending me on a never-ending cycle again. I'm happy I was able to keep it moving.

It's best for me to stay single and rebuild, before opening up to a rebound relationship. Therefore, I've decided to take this time to work on my spiritual and emotional growth. The new goal is to become a wiser woman. I'm still not healed and some days are low, but I'm certainly getting stronger.

PROVERBS 12:22
"Lying lips [are] an abomination to the LORD: but they that deal truly [are] His delight."

Summary

"All relationships are not meant to stay. As a matter of fact, most of them are only for a season so let it go; stop crying." - TD Jakes.

Legendry was selfish. He made sure he was winning before he shut me down. I'm not even sure if they care about the pain he left in my life.

When he was depressed and left alone, during his solitary confinement, they all left him and I picked him up. Now, they all turn against me for fighting back. As women, I was hoping they would be different and understand what a man can do to another woman, but I guess that's not possible.

Maybe they hated me all along. Deception has a way of showing up. "Instead of confronting my disappointment, I'm learning how to live around it." – Sarah Jakes Roberts

We can entertain deadly thoughts that will produce graves for us. I was drowning in anger. I lowered my standards and fought some unnecessary battles, which I should have allowed Jehovah to fight for me.

Bitterness and depression have no place in my life. I am Chosen. I now realize why this thing had a hold on me. It's because I wasn't in my rightful place. I needed to build a relationship with The Almighty God and learn how to love me – all of me.

It was okay not to be okay. However, what was not okay was choosing to make the situation worse. Emotions are also a tool Satan can use against us. Sometimes, it's best to step back and allow things to take its course. Don't be so quick to react. If I had thought things through, the outcome would have been different. In the end, all things work for our good, so there's something I had to learn from this, even though I messed it up.

If I wasn't in my thoughts and emotions that day, I would have never made that call to the prison warden. Legendary might never forgive me, but I must take responsibility for my actions. I really don't believe he will become humble and see his flaws in this since he does demonstrate some narcissistic qualities. In reality, we both taught each other a life lesson. I bet you he won't use another woman and I won't ever trust a man blindly again. Alisha probably got a good man since I helped to prepare him for her.

According to Legendary prison is an ugly thing though, He do not believe it's a great tool in reforming a person. In fact, he stated the gangs, the bullies who force their lifestyles or agenda on others, drugs, and other situations they face in there can make or break a person. He told me some guys are gay in there and then go home and live normal lives with a wife as if it never happened.

After all is said and done, I came to the conclusion that most of my pain was embedded in the lack of acknowledgment. If Legendary would have admitted he done me wrong, the pain would have been easier for me to cope with. I've learned in this case, however, that an apology may never happen.

In essence, I don't even know what to pray for. I'm depending on Jehovah to guide me. But silently, I really want to ask the Almighty God to bring him back to me. I left Legendary, but I was hoping for another chance. He wrote in his last letter, "Angel, you lied to yourself." I know now he was right. I didn't know how much he meant to me before all of this happened. I'm not happy yet, but I know the day will come when I will be free.

You know they say to be careful what we pray for. I asked Jehovah to remove anyone or anything from my life who's not for me. God delivered my request and now I'm here crying. Maybe this is my blessings in disguise. Sometimes, things are not for us and many times, the timing is wrong. I trust you, Lord. You will fix it and fix me.

At forty-four, I'm still single. It's frustrating at times, but I'm still free to find the right person while others are living a sad married life. I always say no one knows when you're going to die, so how do they know when it's your time?

One preacher said you're not married because you're not single. There is no room for your husband since you're still attached to the previous failed relationships. I think she is right - most of us need a detoxing period.

As we all know, nothing hits Jehovah by surprise, so the real question should be why He allowed it to happen. He removed people for a reason so my goal is to run on and see what He has in store for me.

Daily Diary

As I reminisced, I could say Jehovah warned me one day as I was writing him, back in 2016. I felt the Holy Spirit saying this is all a lie. Naturally, I rejected that thought and convinced myself that the risk was worth taking.

I'm not sure how to let go of my past. While others seem to be moving on, I feel stuck. I'm haunted by my experiences, and they keep affecting me as if it was just yesterday. I believe I love Legendary, but that's useless since he doesn't love me back. I felt like he used me since I was available, and the pain is excruciating. He trusted Alisha enough to let her know all my pain and now she's laughing at me. He didn't protect me - he protected her. Why did I allow myself to be used by this man? The one who I reached out to for comfort betrayed me. I placed myself in this position.

I'm too nice, or even a bit stupid. It's clear I have to let go, but it's also clear that I don't want to. I need him and I want him because he completed my happiness. Now my heart is shattered and all I can remember are the words he said to me. "Angel, it has nothing to do with you being ugly. Nothing like that at all. The man who gets you will receive a good woman." That day as he was speaking, I burst into tears and I began thinking, all this time, he felt I was ugly? Since then, he has not spoken to me.

He's now in confinement and he's clearly in love with an ex-felon and not me. Why did he choose to accept her and not give me a second chance? Yes, I tried to walk away, but I wanted him back. Was this love, or was I just being unfair?

Either way, he wasn't supposed to trick me into believing he needed me when he was already building a relationship with Alisha. It seems as if this was a revenge move on his part. It feels like he was never in love with me. I was his help, but not his future, so the first chance he got, he ran with it. At least, that's how I feel, and it hurts deeply. I'm the one who actually reconnected them because I totally believed his lies.

May 17, 2019
I don't know if he wrote me back, but I didn't receive any response to my last letter, although I feel like my mail isn't safe because I have a horrible mailman. However, I continue my life with the expectation that he will write back. Don't misunderstand, I have options out here, but none of them felt right. I hate myself too much to ever trust anyone again.

One of my prospects always has excuses and the pain I feel now only blocks me from seeing any good in him. Maybe I'm wrong, but this is how I feel. The other prospect seems to be taking advantage of the opportunity. I trusted and confided in him about Legendary and it seems as if all he wants is sex and no relationship. Therefore, he too must go. I can't allow myself to be used again, and I'm glad we never started.

Moving on is also a drag. I'm empty inside and feel like there is no reason to love or live anymore. My chest hurts, my head is filled with sad memories, and my mind is in a constant battle with the "what ifs". I want him back, but is that the solution, or is it just a bandage?

I have my daughter, who is so great and makes me proud. I have my dad, but he is more of a burden some days, and I can't leave him to start my own life. After all, I got pregnant at twenty-two and sacrificed my life just so I can be there for my child. Now I felt like it should be my time, and it is not happening

I used to be happy and I was looking forward to my freedom. It feels like my sentence is unfair. If so, what rules did I break? To me, it feels like I did my best. I am a good mother. I've done the best I could. Maybe this is what good people have to face in life.

I can't do half of the things many single forty-four-year-old women can do. Sleepovers, drink, have sex with who I please. My mom raised me as a Christian and that too did me little to no good. I've seen some who slept their way to the altar while they passed me by in life and are happy and now blessed with a husband.

Here I am, still trying to play by the rules. The rules that didn't work for me after all these years and I have no joy. But in reality, they say it's all a trick of the enemy. Guess he did a mighty good job at tricking me because my pain and disappointment are real!

May 18, 2019
I've admired Legendary since high school. He was my brother's best friend. This hurt me so badly, I tried slashing my wrist. I don't even know how to do that suicidal stuff so I failed at that too. Isn't Lucifer a

liar? Legendary even told Alisha all my physical and mental struggles and she threw it in my face. It didn't matter, though. I wanted him back and I kept telling him that, but he didn't want me. Maybe he never did and all I was, was a help to him.

May 19, 2019

My daughter's graduation day was bittersweet. With everything going on, I couldn't even enjoy it the way I wanted to. Yes, I was super proud of her. She did it! A SUNY graduate with Honors. However, my life was in shambles and I was a complete mess.

My daughter wanted her grandpa to be there for her big day, but I knew it would have been hard. It's no fun pushing a wheelchair and being a CNA when everyone else is having fun. Legendary was also on my mind. He'd really treated me poorly, so I was also worried about that. He asked me to do too much, and I kept giving him what he wanted until I got tired of being used. I no longer cared about anything, so I told his sister everything More than likely, no one will believe what I'm saying since I'm just now coming forward with this. However, I'm done covering for him so I choose to say my piece. Now that he wants Alisha, it's not okay for me to protect him anymore - that sneaky ass man.

May 20, 2019

I came back home from Albany and as soon as I entered my yard, I felt anxious about me not having any letters from him. It's either the postman messed up my letters, or he didn't write me back. It had been over two weeks since I sent him a letter, and I have yet to hear from him. My episodes came back and I refused to pray because I was tired. I didn't see any changes, so where were my prayers going? I felt confused, sad, and disappointed. I imagined hurting myself again. My daughter didn't care, she was in her room and she walked away when I snapped at her. She doesn't understand my pain. After all, it was her graduation week so she was super excited.

We just came home from a trip. I was mentally sick and my head hurt. I couldn't even breathe well, but I had to undress my dad and clean him. Then, I had to find time to take care of me. It may not seem like a lot, but it was overwhelming, especially after having a long day.

I want to live again, just like any other person my age. This burden is too much and my days are mundane and predictable. Wake up, get ready for work, return home, and cater to my dad. There's no end - just a never-ending cycle. I want a good life, and I want to be free. Unfortunately, I'm now doing a second term of caretaking, because I'm trying to be a good daughter. Who's going to take care of me?

May 21, 2019
I'm disappointed and in tears. I was expecting this day to be amazing. Recently, I heard a pastor say in twenty-one days, God is going to shift things in my life. On my twenty-first day, I laid awake at 11:19 pm with nothing good to look forward to. Yes, I have life and a job, but what I want I don't have. My life is still stagnant and I'm stuck on this road of confusion. Legendary didn't even write me back and that hurts. The idea of being uncertain haunts me. I want to be happy but it seems like that's a long way from where I am now.

Every day, I think of him. He has a few more days in confinement. I'm not sure if he will call me, but a part of me is excited about that. I don't want to argue with him, but there are a few things we have to work out immediately if this is going to work as a friendship. I'm not sure how to live anymore and loving someone new is impossible right now because I refuse to open up. Men are assholes, including him. I was having an episode, lying in bed, overthinking and talking to myself. It's the new me and I can't seem to stop. I get some form of satisfaction when I do it. I've stopped caring. This allows me to not expect anything. I won't hurt if I don't care.

May 31, 2019
I had my moments of anger and disappointment with Jehovah. Then, I quickly humbled and crawled back to my place at His feet. I need Him. He's my God. Sometimes, I get impatient and refuse to believe in Him. It's like a spiritual tantrum and only a loving God would understand my stupidity.

I cry almost every day and have regular thoughts of dying, of giving up and quitting. Then, at that same moment, I find the desire to live. I guess I'm a bit scared of my future, so it's best to end it now instead of living through the unknown.

As I sit in my room watching the Sarah Fawcett show on DVR, my mind is racing. I'm having constant thoughts of marrying my prison love who I just lost since I decided to walk away from being with him. I realize I needed him more than I thought. This man completes me in a strange way. Some will not understand my type of crazy, but waiting twelve years for him was certainly the plan.

My mind is still racing and trying to control my thoughts is becoming more and more difficult. I remembered the one time my stepdad drove our car into a trench. We had to walk out of the water. I was scared for my life that day, and it's a feeling I will never ever forget. I also remembered my ex who stalked me for a year, and he threatened my life and my family. I remembered my brother who tried to penetrate me at twelve and I was scared Mommy would put him out of the house so I lied when she asked me. These are the types of days I have and why I cry almost every day. I want to be happy again. I'm tired of being at my lowest point.

June 3, 2019
I came to a sad awakening point in my situation. I'm holding onto the past and it's only blocking my future blessings. Pastor Dharius Daniels spoke about releasing your Saul for Paul. God has greater for me and I'm too busy looking back and holding on to what could have been when Jehovah is showing me what greater plans He has for me.

There is a tiny part of me that's hoping my Saul (Legendary) could indeed be changed as Paul did in the Bible story. Saul used to persecute the Christians before God took him and created a believer out of him. He was changed and washed in the blood. Then he became one of the chosen ones to work in the vineyard for Jehovah. Can this be my story? Can Legendary change and be a better man, or would God just replace him with someone new?

June 4, 2019

I spent some time with my dad and my daughter. Later, I listened to love songs that allowed me to think of being in a better place with him. I'm still in a confused state where I want him back, but I'm also trying to let him go. Letting him go will ease the pain while holding on to what I want allows me to find false hope. In reality, I'm not sure that it's over and I'm not sure if he still wants us to be friends. Would I support his bad habits and make it worst? Or would my being in his life help him to stay out of trouble since he won't have to borrow or ask anyone else for anything? I'm not sure, but all these random thoughts keep haunting my soul.

June 9, 2019

I went to Brooklyn Tabernacle and it was awesome. I felt happy and free. God will see me through. I had a few bittersweet moments today. I think of Legendary a lot. I miss him and I still feel like I need him. He makes me happy and he completes me. On one YouTube video, Pastor Dharius Daniels taught that no one should complete you. They can complement you, but only Jehovah should be allowed to complete us.

Even though I had a productive day, I'm not happy now and I'm trying to convince myself that I can move on without him. It's a sad situation. I feel like he loves me, but he clings to Alisha because I abandoned him. I abandoned him because she is a manipulating woman and I fell for her trap. All things will work out the way Jehovah wants it to be. Maybe He will bring him back, or maybe I'll find happiness in someone else. I don't see it, but only God knows.

June 11, 2019
Legendary probably confused the money and attention I gave with love. I am typically a loner, but I loved the idea of having someone who I thought wasn't going anywhere. I felt like he would never leave me. Sadly, after I didn't live up to all his demands, and threatened to leave, that cost me the relationship. The hardest part is moving on and releasing him. Each morning, I wake up with him on my mind and he is the last person I think about when I go to bed. I'm so sad and empty, I don't know what to do. I'll have to keep praying and trusting Jehovah.

June 13, 2019
The psychiatrist recommended meds for my issue. I really don't like taking meds, but I'm at that stage where I feel like I have to do something different. I tried praying and being positive, but that wasn't enough. Legendary still didn't call me and I'm trying to stay positive. I can't help but to think of him being married or something. Part of me will never recover if he does. I also keep hearing Jehovah telling me two years – just wait. That thought or belief didn't help or comfort me because I wanted to know the end while I was still dealing with the process.

I messed up on a few things. I didn't show him enough love and patience. To be honest, I don't know how to love, especially while I'm battling anxiety, depression, and emotional stress. I also feel like he likes money, so he took the highest bidder. Maybe they deserve each other since they walked the same road in this life. The fact is, Jehovah rules in all situations.

June 16, 2019
Why? Legendary betrayed me, so I betrayed him. That cell phone was contraband, after all. He couldn't get away with playing me.

Fair is fair and I'm cleaning out my closet. I wish them well. Secure us and JPAY is closed, so we're going to keep it this way. May God bless him. I still love him, but I'm no longer in love with him. At least, so I think.

June 25, 2019
I didn't write for some days. Maybe I'm getting stronger. I'm moving on. No more stagnant life for me. Over that short period of time, you got about $4,000 from me. Well, I got my heart broken, and I was used. So thank me for sixty days in confinement. Sail safely and be blessed.

Today, June 26th
I failed a big test since I went on an unnecessary tantrum fighting Alisha's sister, DeeDee, instead of her. After all, we were all Facebook friends at one point. I had access to her sister's Messenger account and I spoke my peace, only for us to go back and forth. I tried keeping it clean while she called me every name in the book.

Instead of praying, I wanted to make someone angry because I was angry as well. As they say, misery loves company. I was at work serving my customers and the tears wouldn't stop flowing. At this point, I decided to FIGHT.

DeeDee actually confirmed that he used me and then dismissively, she said, "So what?" Well, one can say she's an example of a good woman. Maybe all that money I was sending him, he was sending it to those broke Florida chicks.

Or since Alisha had felony charges, it was a match made in heaven. Maybe she will do the things I won't do. God chose someone he could relate to.

That's all I had on her - she was a fat felon. She was just as sneaky as her man, so I used it any time I got the chance. Again, I'm miserable so I kept starting trouble with them. This only prolonged my healing and affected my health. One day, I had an epiphany that if I wanted to regain my health and strength, I needed to stop!

When I came home, I actually made a vow to never go there again. I then wrote him on JPAY so clearly, I failed the test of no contact. But I'm going to win in the end since I'm moving on to better things. I'm going to love again. I also decided to deactivate my Facebook page since clearly, it was becoming a distraction. I have to focus on Jehovah and rebuilding my life and allowing Him to fix me and to fix it.

All I am doing is making things worse when I try to fix it myself. I was trying to depend on someone else as a source of my love when my love comes from the Lord, it was a bad decision. Mentally, I'm tormented by these memories but I believe in myself. I believe what Jehovah has in store for me is greater.

www.ingramcontent.com/pod-product-compliance
Lightning Source LLC
Chambersburg PA
CBHW040202100526
44592CB00001B/10